Let Live

by

Eithne Strong

Acknowledgements are due to the following publications in which a number of these poems first appeared: Poetry Ireland Review, North Dakota Quarterly, Connacht Tribune, The Salmon, Songs of Living, Wildish Things, Innti, Comhar, WEB, Orbis, Riverine, The Irish Times, Four Quarters, Krino

❧❧❧❧❧❧❧❧❧❧❧

Cover painting by Graham Knuttel
Designed and Typeset by *nova print*, Galway
Printed by Colour Books, Dublin
Photo by Paul Goulding

❧❧❧❧❧❧❧❧❧❧❧

ISBN 0 948 339 33 0 Hardback £8.50
ISBN 0 948 339 34 9 Softback £4.50

❧❧❧❧❧❧❧❧❧❧❧

Produced with the financial assistance of
The Arts Council (An Comhairle Ealaíon)

❧❧❧❧❧❧❧❧❧❧❧

Salmon Publishing
Auburn, Upper Fairhill, Galway

Contents

Let Live

They had discovered this bit of Ireland
and, although shrewd, adored; it was
their Grail, their Ganges, hill of Olivet,
somehow idealised focus
of their travelled hearts,
still searching
from inside
their earthwatch shapes
- no meat, no nicotine -
of alternative culture.

They had searched the four ends
until finding this late scrag of rock
and heather where they settled.
The knowing locals savoured their oddness
- blow-ins, better than TV, three dimensional;
their sweat lodges and naked capering
under the moon were marked with prurient
spasm from behind furze bushes,
became the stuff of slippery yarns.

However, since astuteness
was on both sides,
the blow-ins took
the local measure
and laughed

at their own imagined ridicule:
they envisaged a permanent sojourn
and laughing
was to mutual advantage.

They asked me what do poets
carry in their pockets.
I said
I could answer only for myself:
this time of year it was bound
to be lavender heads whereupon
I showed them. They were pleased
and I was invited to drink lassi
and later furze blossom wine.

Folding Doors

For the time of day, the sudden small sounds
through the folding doors were unusual -
TV Europe or an unprecedented Gaeltacht feature?
Too soft to know. Attractive though.
Getting up from the struggling page -
legitimate distraction - I went to inspect.

And there I saw him in the window corner,
arms high, salaaming towards the east.
"What on earth......!"
"I'm saying my prayers," he said.
It is a various house: people appear -
there are entrances.

I knew him years. A man for certain spaces.
A deviant from desktops, he had his codes.
His boots in the hall were mountainy.
And now? Later, over yesterday's cold spinach pie,
he filled me nine months' news.
Irish still, always that, but Catholic no more.

Now, a studied convert: "The only faith, you see
not to support usury, the root of all sin."
New to me, this, but I'm learning every day.
"The sufis," he told me, "are the answer."
"How does your wife - staunch woman - feel?"
"Pleased at my improved behaviour."

3

"And your sons?" "Some disapproval - I can
now have three more wives, you know."
I wondered about stamina - he was not young -
and more, money: his eccentric spaces,
expecting the rewards of deviance,
had always been hand to mouth.

Doubtless he envisaged waged wives;
the Prophet's view on these I did not ask.
Instead, "What about Salman Rushdie?" I queried.
"Could be in the mountains here...." said he.
Mind you, he didn't look the one to do it but then
last year, neither did he look headed for Islam.

The Learning Process

We learned new things from him,
our travelling companion,
a man so previously engrossed
in very private occupation
he had not learned
what everyone surely knew
through daily osmosis:
he therefore remarked with wonder
at the carrying of a new baby
in a frontal sling by its father;
the sworn-original type of pancake place
so general these days;
the folding of a napkin
around a wine neck to prevent drips.

When challenged on this last
ridiculous ignorance, he said,
a shade defensively,
that in his background
wine would not anyhow have been
"house" wine and waiters would
anyhow have poured it for one,
the napkin being rather
over their arm than around
the bottle-neck.

There was an adjustment
of holiday protective covering
as we turned to smile, revised,
our mocking mutual armour.

Peanut Queenie

When you go a very long journey
with friends in their car
it is necessary to play your part.
You must bring supplies
to keep things going:
small talk, some of them,
the appropriate noises
at novel sights in the landscape,
a constant level of enthusiasm
for conveniences made available,
the obligingness or otherwise
of the weather et cetera, et cetera.

It is a very tiring necessity,
this furnishing of supplies.
At the end there is considerable comfort
in not having to exclaim about it all,
the endless beauty of the scenery
having become merciless.
After seven hundred miles
and mannerly enquiry,
they tune into pop radio
and contrary to earlier convictions
you find you love Peanut Queenie,
The Queen of the Dancing Floor.

Unapprehended

Dark song arose.
Black
out of the black clefts
borne out of the rocks upheaved jag.

Primeval, before any knowing,
holding the balancing stars;
out beyond the rim of things,
beat dark song.

Old song.
Before ever was life
was the beat of song,
first beat of the life thought.

Strong heavy beat,
to shatter through my flesh now
and shake to wrenching sobs
what holds the shape of me.

Beat on beat
where is life is beat
of old sadness going back
and back and then on and on.

Forces - North Kerry

Curlew-cry:
some old sorrow
always rises
out of the wistful earth
at the curlew's passing.
Sad power of old mountains.
Ancient sorrow swells
on the lonesome dark,
clouds folding down
by the lone lake side.
Old pain rears
out of the pagan past
and I am cleft
with sweep of pagan sorrow
that is such pristine joy
by the lake's lone side
when the curlew cries.

To My Mother

Just before sleep last night
I remembered.

Little woman
bearer of big men.

And before sleep
with knowledge near to tears
I knew again your fight.

Saw
the tired body sit so straight
while hands went on mending
into the late night.

Saw
the weary head
yet firm because of the strong will
bend over books that had to be known
for school on the morrow.

Knew
with surer knowing
your unflinching wrestle
with careful spending
of the much-earned wage.

Remembered
the special care of little things:
for grace of summer curtains
or flowers gathered in still busy
interlude from imperative chores -
remembered, now humble, and with praise.

Remembered too
the slight body in vivid action
against encroaching weeds,
impotently militant against
frequent defeat by horse and cow
in your limited domain.

As mothers live, and see
their children pass from them,
unknowing, I knew your grief.

And now
on hearing great music
tears run and run
for this and this.

I have lived these years
and know but now
pain of mothers
amid their children's going.

The Three who Went

Now they are gone:

The boy who was beautiful -
flower skin, aureole of copper hair,
young thoughts marvelling -
he went from us lonely
on a golden day
one warm September.

The other grown to man of bitter heart,
open only to these bogland ways; held soul
whose only freedom was among these hills,
whose stricken love no people loved
but those who breathed his mountain air -
he went upon an Easter Day.

And then from every mountain reach
they came and came,
along the old rough roads
they came in lines to see
him rest to whose cares
he had so signally seen.

Now the third, the father of the two,
who loved us all if awkwardly.
The people tell, along the hills,
the old rough roads,

about the brown turf fires:
'The Master is dead.'

So now once more they come,
from every reach they come -
and children from the school -
to honour rest.

It is September
and the years have passed
two by two until twenty-two
from that other warmer day.

There they lie,
beneath the stone the boy,
by his right hand the brother
and by his left the father.

Troth

As I would walk to rocks
forever challenging
my secret strengths
I walk to meet you;
margin giants
on the towers of eternity
call me on:
I would always go -
out to your stript eyes
where deceit is not;
to the climbing heights
where is our mating;
to unrealised aeons
where powers of worlds are.

Lover on His
(In response to Black Marigolds)

My love has gone out from the field,
she, the beautiful one,
who wore the wine tresses
and all the grasses were long
and soft about her body.
The easy foldings of her limbs
were fragrant amid the clover.
I loved this girl,
this white one.

Now she has gone, there is a strange
peaceful sorrow like the quiet nightfall
or the liquid balm of twilight;
it is at the beauty of her going
for, as she was, so she went
under the feathered trees
and the buttercups seemed never richer
than they were in the dusk where she went,
this quiet graceful one.

Her long arms bound about me
folding a hush upon my being; I cried
at the sweep of life in easy pulses
over the meadows, full and deep
in the wide swell of the bending grasses.

And she was like honey, was luxuriant
all about my nakedness
as the abundance from the sun
upon the mellowing fields.

The quiet presence of flowers was with us,
slow dusk of June coming out of the sky
while yet the time was golden
with the gentle flowing of the sun.
She, the lovely one.
We drank of each other in the hollows,
the white day's mist delicate
against the distances: we were
the enchanted ones, hearing no sound.

And now, even though she has gone,
my love, trailing out of the fields,
I am strong with the incense of the gold day
about my heart and going down into my feet.
The white body that is hers
remains pure against my nakedness;
and I shall take her again in the shadows,
in the warm waves of the laden air:
I am leaving the darkness now to go to her.

Cycle

To show how strong, he strikes the air:
"Today I'll walk six miles - tonight that work
I *will* finish..." and then he finds the chair.

There where joy of birds is merciless
he sits by the window, wide
to their implacable ecstasy.

Not at all ready to go, "I so
love life," he says, angry with it
for leaving him, its unstoppable urge

in birds. "I so want life," he says,
impotent at its irrevocable continuance
that is to pass him by while, indifferent

to his longing, it impels birds to state
their ordained claim and he not at all
ready to go to his inevitable ground.

It is still too soon for a grand acceptance,
reasoned certain snow and lifeless birds,
perspective of further rapturous impersonal springs.

Gaspé to Ottawa

That was Wednesday and after days
we were coming back,
the evening sending up its warmed haze.
On our right a track,

a brittle sweep of acceptable gold:
the sun across that river
wide as a sea. I, queerly sad,
felt, improbably, a leaving. Goodbye river.

Vast, old, so old; it said what it said:
I would have liked a long flow
of the impossible - our driver sped -
to know what, to know.

Our driver sped. I was thinking
- illogical knife - Is it the last time
for this and this (you sleeping)
the last time?

And then your sleeping was a threat.
Unimpressed, but plainly vulnerable you were,
not having been able to simulate
a constitution remaining in interested gear.

Drained by such persistent panorama,
you did not see nor care

that we were coming back this different way
with, on our right, the splendid water.

Following us always on the left, repeated flight
of silver things, flashing an imaginable history -
silo towers, thin spires, new roofs - their light
the aluminium glint of Canada.

Its dark force of northern heights was cobwebbed later
and queerly sad. The river had said
what it said. I, remembering now, know nothing better:
not this nor this... and now you are dead.

Another Reality

Out of the dark night
morning came
with light so rare
that we were lifted up.
Out of the aridity
of our state happened
a great leap to this light
and a cry went up
out of hearts released
from a long barrenness.
The desert time was over.
Now there would be
a time of great fruitfulness.
The locked mind would open
and the gold pour out
more liquid than the gold
of the earth, not hard,
not clogged in dross,
but pure. Now would be freed
the upward urge, flowering
occur out of the hard past.
These are the days of hope,
courage out of the secret ache,
the sustained mind,
the lifted being,
the days of strong fulfillment.

However Long that Dark
(From the original Irish 1989: Dá fhad an Oíche)

Today will be black night
and pain will spear each pulse -
I know it;
the dark tunnel on and on -
this I understand;
life that is as death for you -
I feel it.
I know, understand, feel,
because so it was for me
a like stretch of time;
by this I am marked
so that now with utter sureness
I can urge you, beloved human,
to search out your courage;
even if the bitter stone
in your chest is, you think,
for ever
and you can take no more,
hold fast, hold fast:
that stone will melt,
the tunnel will become
a flow of discovery
and it will be again morning -
I have seen it.

Progenitors

For some unknowable reason
memory is at its unpredictable doings
and you are suddenly there
in my crowded morning.

On this capricious summer day
why's and why's in new questionings
query unaccountably in my head.
I didn't really know you, Dad.

Just loved you. I think: soon
I will reach the span of your years
and how unknown, in sum, you were,
I am, is anyone, at the end.

We bury, burn, turn from cemeteries,
crematoria, resuming the necessary banal
but you, all the rated dead, eclipsed
by clay, waters, do not die.

Irrevelant to our usual capers, you are
suddenly back: a look, a quality, the answers
still missing and, in the self-important busyness,
somewhere a cry, a long longing.

Would Jonathan to David?

I will never go to see you now
not trusting anything about myself;
the time for not trusting you is
over, past because such ruined faith
had meaning only in her connection -
she who, still explaining, died.

Were I to visit, it might be I went
attempting proof: to you, to me,
the ill had healed
no rancour left;
to prove how fine I am
at handling situations.

I am not.
The wound is there,
raw, unappeased, always.

I attempt to skin it over,
try the remedies, wrap
it up, go out to work,
talk, meet,
attempt a pace as if
there were no severed thing.

There is: the thing that was
the heart of us, us - the she-me,

lifetime whole - is knifed quite off.
In the night the cutting sears
piercing thin sleep, convulses
brain by day, no warning when.

I will never go to see you now,
not trusting anything about myself -
no warning what.

The Year of the Grass
(From the original Irish 1989)

This year the grass got
the better of me;
it has not stopped growing
since March
and I've been sweating like
a pig, struggling
with my bockety lawnmower.

I was thinking I might get a break
around July - a dry spell,
possibly, but each day rain came
bringing on the growth,
and then again as to August,
that was
the wettest August of the century.

Come Autumn, I thought, the grass
will be tired, it will rest,
go to sleep. But not a bit of it:
September, October -
they were the sunniest months yet,
just the odd shower which
the grass sucked down, then sprang.

Today, November Day, the air is soft;
I open doors, sunshine amazes

the passage sullen a moment since;
outside, Autumn steals about:
leaves, as wings, float, to settle gently
their yellow on the grass
which is vivid, thrusting like the Spring.

The White Dress
(From the original Irish 1989)

I set behind me
all that happened
resurrected once again -
death and the grave twice already -
I felt the bind in my face
and set it free
my mouth laughed
and I put on a white dress.

I welcomed
the brightness
gathered up
a great armful
of primroses
their fragrance moved with me
all along the road.

The old black ghost of me
was lurking behind a tree
I turned fully towards it
my mouth wide wide
laughing.

When it returned
the following night
threatening suddenly

from a corner of the room
I gave it the same treatment.

Now at last
ah at last -
was not the dark long and bare? -
since I have on the white dress
the black ghost is powerless:
see me fleeting
to the bright field.

The Giant's Causeway

Where the giant was we too are here,
that mighty he, sprung huge from
the imagination of emergent men
to signify a yearned-for power.

They, longing to master the deadly threat
of elements, beasts, other men, saw
the causeway as his stepping-stones athwart
a swallowing sea, to him their shallow feat.

With new views now, we see molten power
cooled to enduring prism: it witnesses to giant
still, just barely held beneath the front,
the shell of earth, daily face of me and you.

Bloody Foreland

Sponsored meagrely they came, eager,
the London students, extending to all deprived
their working fluency. After Bogside, Derry,
they came to view how Donegal contrived
- in their hired mini bus- with kelp and dole
and fish and grants, old settlements redone
to modern demands: stuff for the whole
diploma thesis. In the parlour, fun

with the foxy priest, whiskey and lulling turf;
nothing deprived. Before dusk they bunch
by Bloody Foreland, squaring to the rough
change, taking photos: themselves against March
sky, the furious cliffs, the madder seas.
The Land of Youth, one says, breathing the storm
on top of whiskey. The white mares
gallop endlessly to the shore.

Achill

City people get lost here, drawn
into measureless seductions;
Mweenaun twilight takes their senses,
the slender magnet of a young moon;

they even leave a lover's bed to watch
the dark turn day above Slieve More.
Light is in command here, dictating behaviour
to holiday folk, ruling deluge,

determining the turn of shark and seal,
the hours of gale. But this place
of light and spell does not really grace,
compelled away in cold centuries people,

those who came to live. Its lures
assured in ageless age, there it
waits, laughing its light,
avenging on later men its scars.

Beara Peninsula

There we are. See us now, high. Shock:
we cling, clutch in the bladed furze.
Fastnet far, flung on a foaming rock
in a wide empty water - a kind of fear:

that foaming band pulls down -
look up! that empty sea
charged full from wind and moon
compels our eye - oh up! look up!

What are we doing here with our mouths
laughing like the yellow gorse,
our skin in ecstasy as heather curves
to the windy clouds?

Barrow Estuary

Talk about the Barrow Estuary
and I'll see Strongbow and McMurrough's Aoife
wedded in the streets flowing blood.
For so to our child-mind it was told.

We carried Norman genes, loved atrocities,
while frightened at our leaping brutal relish.
Much older, with approved manners, we were guests
in a stronghold on those easy Barrow swards.

Travel firms pronounced it the sunniest corner
and though crops swelled on this alluvial cover
and Dermot, Strongbow, Aoife fed less imagination,
Bretons cycled past, hawking strings of onions.

Dublin Bay

A good time to come is January:
there is a geranium sky behind Longford Terrace,
a black pine gone mad between chimneys,
from where you stand by the abandoned soap factory.

Turn right: the town is walled in mist;
no twentieth century, but hard, sure,
the winter rip of Vikings, tearing dire
by Howth, fogged also, yet solid, fast.

You are back where Brian seemed holy,
praying in Clontarf. There are no bulls either
nor the strewn excesses of a modern summer
at Seapoint. Only the cormorants, happy,

and the ceaseless pagan sea; you climb
as do two or three others, each alone,
trudging towards that queer geranium zone...
January, there, is a good time.

Henrietta, Caleb and Issue

A squat shape, Hetty,
nourished on a budgeted supply
of Wicklow stew
which was, depending on your view
helped out with sausages
or embellished with them:
not browned first
- a waste of fuel, that -
they remained pig pink and swam.

Salt of the earth, her tight community,
all solid principles seriously applied, in poor supply
joy - laughing, a serious matter also its roots:
they had to be solidly held, no bubbling hoots
nor unhinged yells, no mad flight of the ridiculous.
Laughter, in fact, required a licence:
limited duration, restricted areas
only, controlled pitch and volume,
salvation likeliest reached with a frown.

Over forty, Hetty was twenty years a member when
Caleb - newcome from Wales, a widower then -
joined the Walkers' Club. After
careful months, they walked to the sensible altar.
Serious gardeners, they had still time for one fruit;
indeed two grew; each, in time, and nourished
on salutary economy, took prizes, flourished.

Hetty squatly took their praise as her meed,
Caleb's earnest smile said the Lord saw them good.

So Caleb took early retirement, brought
them all to Calgary where had been wrought
a century's solid network of the faith.
Unerringly, Hetty had planned their path
from Wicklow, now established principled contacts
as was her way; sustaining stew continued
and other right practices; joy maintained
a distance; according to foreseeable manoeuvres
she would shortly implement marriages.

However
the prize fruits, earners
of their own
good money,
set up
individual abodes;
then, madly laughing, rose
to proceed with explorations
of unlimited dimensions.

September Song

One of these days I'll take myself in hand, get
some money together and buy a small car that works.
I'm fed up with the discouraging old carcass
crouched by the pavement, its every joint
and muscle geared to misbehave or block -
a surly clogged-up lump, intractable. It is
too like myself. I need a car that will encourage me,
that will, for instance, keep the rear-view mirror
steady and operate with soothing reflex
as do the cars of friends who give me
lifts. I'd like a realistic backward measure:
I tend to put a lot down to the stiffness in my neck.

I'll get my eyes seen to before that.
There are things they can do these days:
there's that laser operation -
gives you the shivers when you think of it
although I know a teenager who swears
by it. Her father had money and didn't shun
the price. She said, securely,
"My Daddy loves me". I have
no Dad and spare money never a bit
but I'll get it together somehow for he's costly,
this tricky eye-man, a defected Slav -
I tend to put a lot down to poor sight.

And in my new car that works,
giving me a true rear view,
maybe I could venture alone this time to Cahirciveen,
attempt long slow ways to Vienna or Aix-
en-Provence, along boreens - they don't know
that word in Europe - for, even
with my new laser view forward
and my steady rear-view mirror, I'll still
need boosting, will wish to keep clear
of all carrier trucks that brute the ground,
ten-wheel furies to suck you in their violent pull
and, like some memories, blast a courage mostly fear.

Hola Verdad!

There is something soothing to the ego
in having before you the puzzled look
of a foreign student eager to learn your lingo:
there you are, for once at a clear advantage,
in entire command, with valuable assets.

You make full use of such a situation;
you are not, understood, a teacher, rather
a creature with pleasanter connotations,
a free giver, with (you fancy) impeccable
enunciation, *and* in a social context.

Granted the social aspect is a little awry,
for you articulate a pace unnatural to your
volatile disposition which, many times, has had
you in jeopardy but then, for that very reason,
the easing of speed is mutually beneficial.

You expound - just a trifle, too much abstraction
being irrelevant and you are, anyway, somewhat
tongue-in-cheek; however, to pontificate thus
minimally, is emollient; you are so unquestionably,
now, the authority: who is to gainsay you?

Enjoying the safety, you proceed, invent,
but do not pretend a lot, just stretch sometimes
the boundaries of your travels, amplify adventures:

you allow yourself such latitude as pardonable
exercise in verbs, especially those hanging on if.

Mainly you stay with objects round about
or those likeliest to be encompassed
in the student's day; you give him valuable
conversational English and warm to the zeal
with which he always puts anxious jottings

in his inside zipped pocket; you like
to imagine him later perusing them
in compliment to your precious bestowal,
committing them to permanence, that is to say
a notebook or, highest value, memory.

You are making your mark,
are impressing as more than adequate,
are, indeed, highly regarded
- all amusing ballast against
your inner facts of self-encounter.

'Counterrevolution'

In remote Trassac, first day,
you stretch your city shape
under the great light
that arcs south
above the massive limestone hang;
a little healing promises your skin
and stays, encouraging hips, knees.

Four successive days you amble
to the hamlet Marcilhac-sur-Célé;
going to buy your baguette,
you find the boulangerie
already almost bare
for the buying is always early
and you are holiday late.

You might meet no-one, see
only the deaf mute, guardian
of the bells, taking it easy
since no tourists; old abbey
walls warm, benign in the sun,
grudges against that Amadour
long lapsed to mere anecdote.

For four sequestered days
no TV, cassettes, radio,
no news, no outside world;

you have been free
from urban filth, thriven
in this rare peace, green air,
profusion of wild buds.

After twilight,
down by the Célé,
the night birds pipe,
each time a single note,
the cliffs holding the pure sound.
On the third night
the moon comes almost full.

Today, paying for your wine,
you include *La Dépêche*
from the pile: local fun, you think,
pétanque and little fêtes -
and then you see
the murdered young, the riddled dead
in Tiananmen Square.

Yellow Joke

I have a great liking
for the ridiculous,
the way it makes
a fatal hole in solemnity,
letting in
the light of laughter.

The sky cracked
and there was a huge laughing.

Lightning ridicules, splitting
pompous clouds, rending
their bloated threat
to the splendid mockery
of thunder,
the elemental hilarity
of crazy rain.

Let us enjoy the banana skin
bringing dictators to the ground.

Thomas Mann Country

You can walk the canal path from Lubeck
to Hamburg and with you all the way go
great poplars; the life span of their kind
I do not know but their giant rustling
seems as news of centuries; the water
carries Baltic lore under their imaged shapes.

In Thomas Mann country trees flourish to rich height,
their drink the lakes, their food alluvium of aeons;
their multiplicity of birds seem not to sleep in June
for, wakeful, you hear them cheep the short night,
chutter until quick light when, transcendently,
they celebrate - an energy of joy, unique.

A generous place: portions pile your plate.
In the Saturday square a travelling troupe mimes
a parody to medieval instruments. Hard by, a simmer
of smoked sausages, a row of mustards - all hot
in a cool June. You eat yours funnelled in bread
by the cathedral wall, decide to move southwards.

The canal stems villages, buildings flower either side;
gardens replicate symmetry, the irregular has, it seems,
no countenance in this land: dawn hears workers on their
scheduled way to responsible field or city hours. Plan
and produce, a positive programme. Sunday, in a burst
of shrubs, the timbered tiny church. Pulled by its age,

you enter, notice dates; variety of ancient patterning
on wood, hand-painted; the brushed and tailored gathering.
You stay to hear. Later, in your white bed, wakeful
as the night-long chutter in the trees, you keep seeing
that savage passion of the preacher who flashed his fist
and yelled at the unanswering assembled faces.

Bald

To endow my emulative compostions
with a global dimension
a universally concerned aura - indeed,
maybe, even extraterrestrial, since
all that space is for agonising -
I have a list of things to put in poems:
you get nowhere these days in the arts
unless you ring convincing
in your urgency to radical reform,
to far-reaching influence.

And yet today, I feel myself
primarily moved to write about
those balding heads.
Not on the list but
for years they have disturbed me
and I have kept reminding myself -
and then forgetting - to put reactions,
nicely crafted, on paper
with just the degree of detachment
to win critical approval.

I am always troubled to see
those unhappy strands compelled
to freakish length athwart the bone, coerced
from their natural home, still-active border
above the ear, or even - unhappier yet -

dislocated from the innate downward drift
of poll and dragged across the scalp,
itself an honourable, often very handsome
manifestation but now mocked, diminished
by such grotesque overlay.

I applaud the exposed dome,
give it special praise,
find it has a dignity; enhances presence;
there are those we know who carry it so.
They have, of course, other baldnesses
they cover as mine do I who wear my thatch
with a difference - that's why I now suggest
to all of us baldies a hanging on to courage,
letting the hair fall as it may: possibly
this rings sufficiently global for today?

Welcome

I have killed countless times.

Killing is too easy.
Dying also.
Living is hard.

At a young age, eight or so,
I castrated a man, a baddie,
sketched execrably
in my brother's cowboy magazine.
I spent a heated hour or thereabouts
doing this, one Saturday morning.
My brother was with my parents:
they had taken him town shopping
in the pony trap, leaving me.

I, fighting to be favourite,
jeopardised all possibility,
contradicted - serious offence -
answered back - another, was called
brazen hussey. Our parents worked
and worked. Once, I sobbed out grief
to the girl - no-one ever said *maid* -
that was for townee snobs
with daughters in lahdedah convents.

The girl did her best,
my parents working
and working,
but I believed myself
unfavoured;
I unwished that self,
wanting to be
as he,
my brother.

The district liked him,
he made it laugh:
he had male scope.
The people prized
his wish to stay;
they took
his lack of push
for loyalty to roots.
He was theirs.

For years
he pushed me down
with fists, feet, words -
no lack there.
I longed for him:
Please like me, my brother.
I never said it.
Instead, I began to make
advantage from my difference.

Hungry, urgent, I outdistanced him,
ate new territory, proved
some femaleship. All so long ago.
Somewhere in the years he inscribed
a book to me: *With love.* Solitary
declaration. I had won.
But by that time
I knew all his fears:
it was no victory.

Now, there are so many dead.
I am tired of competitions,
spend much time with hindsight.
Anyone may visit me.

Liberté, Dublin '89

Rare summer, the guards are down.
There are riots of enthusiastic flesh.
Previously held unsuitabilities appear,
uncensured, all judgment waived. Standards
swivel, allowing general amnesty. Fat secrets
roll about, become confessional. The bus stop
sees the back of truth much wrinkled
in a low-cut scrap. Intemperate shorts
walk dogs and juiceless flanks. Long teeth
go shopping, wearing minimum, easy
in the flop of accumulated mounds. There is
a large relief at relinquished camouflage.
The beach supports alignments, disrobings
alongside total strangers, proximities
scandalous in a winter context. Anywhere,
quite likely, a divinely vulgar statement
of blemished flesh, no longer cowering,
rejected, attempting apologetic disguise.
Meanwhile, around some ruling bodies
there remains the customary fog
and the letter-box, each post, canvasses
for the Senate. Later, there will be
revisions, the knives freshly in place.

Summer Hearing in a Gardening Hat

Doors, windows flung wide.

An old scratchy record player
blasts from the seventies:

In the days when rock was you-ung
me and Susie had so much fu-un...

... but I *love* Earl Grey.

Yes, indeed, agreed but
in the supermarket yesterday
... promotion for Barry's Tea -
10% off *and* a green star voucher
for next purchase - off 15%!

Yes, indeed, yes
but I *love* Earl Grey....

... as the years went by...
Susie left me for a foreign guy....

Need bread, Ma, an' milk?

Yeah, but later'll do...

too hot now ...resting ....

...California grass...
get back to where you once belonged....

Nasturtium chutney! Really?
Must try it....

Don't wallow, child.
remember skin cancer ...
only mad dogs and Irishwomen....

... hoppin' and boppin'
to the Crocodile Rock....

Waters

One Friday night he packed up
and left. That is, he took
the moulting toothbrush
and half the block of soap -

there was some clinging still
of bourgeois grades to his
brave fling, Siddartha, off
to contemplate the Liffey,

so to speak: it might be
any flow, he being open
to the nudges of suggestion.
They pushed him severally.

West, for example, where rivers
rotted fish in effluents essential
to upkeep swank company cars
that honked him sideways.

Nudged dockside, he, misfit, got
done over; the muggers, bored,
raped then a young one
and, for contrast, an old.

Having long run out of soap, become
nearer seamless by further waters,

on the Pont des Arts, he chalked
a picture making no particular point:

enough he needed the money.
They got it, of course, that night -
the *clochards* under the bridge.
He still had an end of bread

but no pinstripe, wife, kids -
his absence cited major aberration
or good riddance: what matter?
He was fulfilling destiny.

Far east, he and morning saw
the maimed shrewdly deposited:
evening their takings reckoned,
their creature value ever dispensable.

The child slaves, chained to work,
took their water, crust, mat, lot;
knowing nothing, powerless utterly,
they were entirely replaceable.

Articulating no outrage, he went
north; regarding snowy springs,
acknowledged sublime impotence:
endlessly reshaping, everything passes.

The Pursuit of Cure

The decade was full of therapies,
ways of escape from so many kinds
of imprisonings. In fact, 'bind'
became a fairly general word;
it had an educated whiff and so
became 'hang-up' in street use or
when the users, if privileged,
wanted to reassure as to their
common humanity, mass sympathy,
immersion in the popular stream -
cliché took on an altered type.
It was good policy to show openness
regarding the variety of mental conditions
preventing the flowering of full potential.

Equate with the masses, help your neighbour
as yourself. Among other processes, these
frequently meant copulation between
unlikely partners. This kind of mutual help
for a while allowed release, a gleeful
revolution, the progeny resulting an ethnic mix,
a class mutation, spit in the face of fuddyduddy.
But, inevitably, a tiring set in,
the therapeutic principles not being proof
to consistent practice or sliding
into newer liberations where wearying

partners could shed, particularly their young.
These, equipped with their inheritance,
ensure a continuing industry.

Summer Seine

On the shrubby end of Isle Saint Louis
you may sit, absorbing. You are
in that suspended solitariness that is
for good and bad in great cities; there,
ignored, ignoring, private, exclusive until -
it is about three-thirty, Friday afternoon -
the increasing madness beyond each river wall
presses in, hearing suffers a lunatic invasion:
the ravening engines attacking ears plus
the obligatory weekend out of town.
Late Sunday, unnourished, will witness
their peevish, nosetail, crawled return.
Watching the easy nod of leaves
in the light river winds,
you re-achieve a thankful deafness,
a relative belief in the good of islands.

Making

The chart showed the sun in one
of its cyclic passions, flinging off
fireballs, flares; against it, mere dot,
the earth, chart black. "Extinction",

they said, "a new hell, it will get us all."
"Not you," we said, "not you nor us; we will
all be long gone in our own brand of scorch:
rivalries, cliques, coteries."

Meantime, the deathless lust to make is full:
see how she, a throbbing twelve, awaits
the monthly seal of power, her small buds
athrust, her lips a knowing scarlet call.

See how he, any age, always hopeful organ,
snuffs, advances, stirrings in the groin.
It will be, despite annihilations: in fine,
because of them? O magnificent why!

Private?

They objected, "These things are private,
you must not write about them." But
privacies are the stuff, the sine qua non
of writers: subtly placed, distanced,
transmuted, tangential - merely being,
they will out whatever shape,
the academicians' boon, ground for beavering.

Pram

Poor as poor, we bought the pram
on the never never - there was
no other way. The cheapest there,
an excuse of a thing. I cannot recall
exact cost, I think twelve quid, a huge
sum for us then and, of course, the interest
brought it up more; always, everything
we had to pay was too much - even so,
sometimes we took a guilty coffee
and a cake at the Roman Cafe.
       About the pram, they
stamped the instalment book - my name,
the mother, more appropriate - each week
but the father paid: we were pledged
partners, did things together. I
hadn't a sou - reasons for that, too.
He paid strictly except
the last bit, the child a year, pram
already wrecking.
There came
       a threatening letter:
certain unavoidable consequences in the event
of nonpayment - a fine or prison. I see my
big mouth, loud, to friends declaring
I would go to gaol. To me, I was
spirited, vocal, making a case against
shoddy goods, usury. I knew, too,

appetite for experience, for keeping up
the fight against background where gaol
was a disgrace - I hadn't thought it out.
        The friends who had
little, were generous: they paid. I must
reassert I was in full earnest but they
said it would harm the child,
also the father in his
skimpy vital job. It would
harm them, too, standing by
and letting happen.
A mean thought, that;
it came later.
        I have since
harmed the child
and the child
and the child ...
there have been so many. And -
is it worse? -
about keeping
my mouth shut,
I have learned much.